WHY RESILIENCE SUCCEEDS WITH GOD!

God's Way of Building Resilience for A Triumphant Life

ROSEMARY UGONO

For enquiries, email: RNUgono@gmail.com

amazon.com/author/www.rosemaryugono.com

Rosemary Ugono

ISBN 978-1-5272-7109-8

WHAT PEOPLE ARE SAYING ABOUT THIS BOOK

This book 'Why Resilience Succeeds with God!' contains not only the heart of Mrs Rosemary Ugono but also the heart of the Father (God) for those going through life challenges. In this unprecedented time where news of hopelessness is the order of the day due to the impact of COVID-19, this book gives assurance, restore hope and confidence in God. It also leads the way to find the heart of the Father in challenging times. Get set for a life changing encounter as you read.

Dr Afolabi Otitoju, Parish Pastor,

RCCG Victory Assembly

Banchory, United Kingdom

This book carefully breaks down what it means to be resilient and exposes the blind spots that are often glossed over when discussing resilience. I particularly enjoyed the aspect that gave guidance about how to make tough decisions. In the author's words, resilience requires that you "deal with your feeling first by getting it under control before going ahead with your actions and decisions". That is very apt as emotions have a way of clouding the mind and often produces sub-optimal decisions under those circumstances. You would want a read of this book – so go ahead and do it. Be resilient, I am sure it will be worth the while.

Dr David Emele, Music Director

RCCG Scotland, United Kingdom

I highly recommend this book to anybody who wants to build their resilience and make life changes in a godly way. This book is an easy to read guide that teaches you and shows you that resilience and diligence is key to achieving success.

Lola Okunrinboye, CEnv

Aberdeen, United Kingdom

Quite an interesting read. You have given your readers a better understanding of resilience.... working hand in hand with diligence. Never seen it like this before.

Mrs Ifeoma Umez

Aberdeen, United Kingdom

Whoa! The book is interesting, motivational and captivating. I am confident it indeed will be a valuable source of inspiration in assisting a lot of people develop resilience towards attainment of self-actualisation. Quite amazing to see how author's inherent literacy prowess was unleashed. Well done!

Winston Ugono,

Project and Risk Management Consultant

Aberdeen, United Kingdom

DEDICATION

I dedicate this book to my dear Son, **David Ugono**.
You are my joy and heritage from God Almighty,
mummy loves you.

FOREWORD

Having known Rosemary for over ten years as a member in our church and an adult Sunday School teacher, I am not disappointed at all at the succinctness and the quality of this book.

The author has drawn heavily from her own rich life experience which were by no means easy, and she has thereby made real what it takes to be resilient. Her openness and candour brings a lot of authenticity to the book.

The first chapter on attitude is a wise opening gambit that is most appropriate. The same Charles Swindoll she referenced in the chapter is famed to have said that *"...Life is ten percent what happens to me and ninety percent how I react to it."* With such a strong opening to the book, it became clear to me very early on that the author has a good grasp of what it takes to triumph over life circumstances.

That attitude only holds in the face of strong character foundation cannot be faulted as she made a strong argument for this most important fact.

The book is very positive and filled with hope, Mrs Ugono did not dwell on the negative but was very gentle and encouraging in her approach. The constant message all through the book is – "you can do it". She did not leave any room for self-doubt as she urged the reader to stay the course as he or she depends on God.

'Why Resilience Succeeds with God' is good news to the ears and sweet songs to the soul. For the author, no mountain is too tall to climb, and no ravine is too deep to cross. Anyone reading this book who is experiencing some difficulties should take solace in the fact that God has promised not to leave or forsake us. This truth remains the central theme of this book - the truth that nothing is too hard for God to take you through and bring you out on the other end unscathed.

This book is a timely message for this generation where everything is fleeting and superficial. Ours is also a generation of instant gratification, and there is therefore no other words of encouragement as needful as the message in this book. As powerfully presented in this book, it is indeed possible to play the long-term game and still win resoundingly.

The highlight of this book for me is the strong submission that Rosemary made; that all said and done, none of what is written will be achievable except through the help of the Holy Spirit.

The Lord Jesus Christ says – "I am the vine, you are the branches. He who abides in Me, and I in him, bears much fruit; for *without Me you can do nothing.*

This book is a great resource that I believe shall remain timeless. Please use it as such and help others to benefit from it.

Dr CHRIS GBENLE - Provincial pastor,

Redeemed Christian Church of God (RCCG) Scotland

United Kingdom.

CONTENTS

CHAPTER 1

Understanding How You Can Be Triumphant

Living a life of triumph is something we all must aspire for in life. Making a change in our realm of existence is important if we must realise the dream of living triumphantly and overcoming challenges and circumstances of life. There are various inner strengths and abilities God has deposited within us. Tapping into these strengths to build resilience and develop winning attitudes for triumphing in life, requires continuous work and trust in the supernatural help of God. Prepare yourself to rediscover these strengths and abilities, skills, hidden knowledge and potentials, recognise them and utilise them to your advantage over the vicissitudes of life. Trust in God's way to help you develop the resilience required for a triumphant living.

1.1 Why I Decided to Write This Book

I decided to write this book for everyone that dreams of triumphing in life, over situations and circumstances. To reawaken their inner strengths, draw from those strengths in developing and building resilience for a triumphant life. Also, for those that are facing some form of challenge in their lives and thinking that there is no way out of it; to encourage them to develop a winning attitude that will not only help them through those challenges, but also linger on even after the challenge is past.

Attitude will shape who you are and what you will become in life. What you will achieve or not achieve in life is dependent on your attitudes. Your attitude is your true nature, who you really are; your true personality. *"I believe the single most significant decision I can make on a day-to-day basis is my choice of attitude. It is more important than my past, my education, my bankroll, my successes or failures, fame or pain, what other people think of me or say about me, my circumstances, or my position. Attitude is the 'single string' that keeps me going or cripples my progress. It alone fuels my fire or assaults my hope. When my attitudes are right, there is no barrier too high, no valley too deep, no dream too extreme, no challenge too great for me"* – Pastor, Charles Swindoll.

Developing the right attitudes for life cannot be overemphasised; these winning attitudes can become a part of our lives, helping us grow in Hope and Faith in God. Right attitude can reduce the gigantic nature of a challenge and help us focus on God, rather than the giant of a situation.

As stated earlier, this book is for everyone that is aspiring of living a triumphant life over situations and circumstances of life, who have made up their minds that failure is not an option they are willing to settle for or live with, those who are tired of the life of mediocre and are ready to go the extra mile or take the next step. Eric Greitens - in his book Resilience, said that *"Those who really go for excellence fail more often than the mediocre people, because the mediocre are so afraid of failing that they never put themselves out there".* Note that failing is not the same as settling for failure. Decide that it is time to be triumphant, time to push yourself towards your dreams by rediscovering your inner strengths and resilience and engaging them to achieve your goals. Look beyond any challenge you are facing now, focus on developing a winning attitude and hope in the mist of that challenge, turn your situations around by desiring on growing in your journey of hope and faith in God.

1.2 Those that will Benefit from This Book

Everyone that have ever dreamed of triumphing over situations and circumstances of life, those that wants to make a change in their realm of existence. Those that are facing one form of challenge in their life will benefit from this book, as well as others that equally think that they do not have a challenge; but just want to develop a winning attitude to life that will help shape their responses to everyday situation will benefit too.

This book is intended to address the pain of all those facing one form of challenge or the other. Those secret questions that we ask ourselves while going through these difficult times, like; why me?, will I ever come out of this the same?, will this mean my end?, how do I cope with this?, does anyone even understand what I am passing through? All these questions I will try to answer in this book. However, look beyond the pain, there is a gain after the pain. Remember that after night comes the dawn.

This book will attempt to fill the gap of hopelessness during challenges, bringing renewed resilience to come out of it with a winning attitude and live a life that triumphs over challenges. Hopelessness is synonymous with inability to try, because one feels that there is no point or the need to try. In life we keep taking steps towards our desired aspirations, irrespective of the challenges in front, we can only get to our dreams if we do not give up and throw in the towel; and this can only happen through resilience, having a winning attitude, trust and faith in God Almighty.

CHAPTER 2

The Message of Hope

My message is that you are capable of triumphing over unfavourable situations and circumstances of life. You have the determination and ability to pull through your challenges from within you. Most times we often look unto the ability of others to help us pull through or conquer our challenges. For instance, when one is sick, it is natural to want to look up to the health professionals for a solution and / or to God. However, there are instances you will need to depend on your inner strengths, determination and resilience in order to surmount your challenges.

Consider the athletes and try to imagine their inner energy and the sheer determination they exhibit despite the prevailing atmospheric and natural circumstances around them. I used to be an athlete in my secondary school days and can relate with the determination and doggedness required in developing and retaining a winning attitude during challenges; thereby resolving to triumph over them. I have learnt to not give up on life or dreams even when it looks blink and you too can search within to find your inner strengths and abilities. Hope will keep your dreams alive, so keep hope alive.

2.1 There Is Hope

From a Christian perspective, depending on the Holy Spirit is the only way to grow your hope and faith during challenging times. I can say this because it has worked for me in numerous occasions. You must learn to depend completely on him as the word of God in Proverbs 3:5 encourages us to trust in God rather than on our own understanding. In other words, you may understand the enormity of the issues facing you, the limited availability of resources on hand to combat the impending or current challenge, yet God wants us to look to Him and trust Him to take control.

2.2 Depend on The Holy Spirit

Consider this analogy, our spiritual walk with God is likened to a people who can see versus a people that are blind and so depends on a guard. The Bible in John 9:41, tells a story about Jesus and His audience. Jesus was speaking to the Pharisees and said to them if you were blind, you should have no sin: but now you say, we can see; therefore, your sin remains with you. In life, when you can see, you are completely dependent on your sight to go wherever you want. Thus, you oversee your affairs, abilities, senses and perceptions. Your achievement then depends on you and how you utilise your sight or natural abilities and there is so much one can achieve by oneself.

However, when you are blind and depend on a guard, whom I will liken to the Holy Spirit, you will need to trust in his supernatural powers and abilities, his leadings and perceptions. You will depend on him for health, wisdom, character, enabling or prevailing environment for your hopes to become reality and for open doors of desired opportunities and destiny helpers; these you may not be able to achieve on your own ability. So, that takes us back to not trusting in our own understanding according to the word of God, but rather to depend and trust in God the Holy Spirit.

2.3 Accept Jesus Christ As Lord and Saviour

If you are not a Born-Again Christian, you will need to accept Jesus Christ as your Lord and Saviour. By saying a simple prayer of repentance to him and asking him to come into your life and begin to lead you from now on. The Bible (KJV) says in Romans 10:10 *"for with the heart man believeth unto righteousness; and with the mouth confession is made unto salvation"*. I once read a book by a Muslim woman, named, Bilquis Sheikh, titled, "I Dared to call Him Father". She recounted her miraculous story from Islam to how she became a believer in the Christian faith by encountering God. Though her journey was not without its challenges, as one would expect, but when we depend on the Holy Spirit, we will always come out triumphant as she did. You too can take a bold step by seeking to know God the Holy Spirit.

2.4 Lessons to Learn When All Is Going Well in Life

Maybe you already have a relationship with God the Holy Spirit and currently do not have a challenge or have never been challenged, now you are wondering what on earth I am talking about. Well I am in that situation too, where everything is sometimes hunky-dory, yet there are numerous lessons to learn when all seems well in life. These life lessons will help us to maintain a winning attitude and build an atmosphere of victory around our successes, thereby helping to shield us from invisible enemies of success.

a) The first lesson is learning to deal with negative pride when all is well with us. It is understandable when we take pride in what we do or things we have achieved in life but going beyond that to becoming proud and headstrong about it, is tantamount to inviting negative forces that works against our successes in life. The oxford dictionary defines pride as "the quality of having an excessively high opinion of oneself or one's importance." The bible puts it in a clearer form, in Proverbs 16:18, *"pride* *goes before destruction, and a haughty spirit before a fall".*

b) Secondly, envy is another thing we must work against when we are succeeding in life. You may want to ask why would anyone be envious if they are already succeeding? Well, it is because success and contentment does not usually go hand in hand. In other words, when all is well, is the time to focus on what is working and build on your principles to continue growing. We can learn from others ahead of us or even request their help or input, to help us think outside the box, however, envy should never be the reason for doing what we are doing.

c) Thirdly, success attracts lots of attention for both good and bad reasons, irrespective of what area of life one is successful. So, being humble will go a long way in dealing with these attentions in a way that is not detrimental to our future successes. Humility in general is a good quality to have, whatever your circumstance in life, it is a winning attitude that guides you from unnecessary errors in life and opens doors of great opportunities with destiny helpers to the humble.

d) Fourthly, when all is going well and we seem to have everything at our beck and call, we would naturally want to satisfy our inner most desires. Especially if we are successful financially, this is when we would require self-control as a winning attitude to protect us from the damaging effects of lack of self-control. Not only in our finances do we need self-control but in all aspects of life, in our character, emotions and appetite, etc. All of which requires a good dose of self-control regularly.

e) Finally, when all seems well in life, we must learn not to limit our selves by ceasing to dream further. It is dangerous to assume that you have reached your zenith simply because you have achieved a level of success in life. Life is dynamic and we must constantly evolve with it by seeking new ways of improvement despite our life's successes and achievements.

CHAPTER 3

Life Can Be Better

Life is precious, it must be guided with care. Having the right knowledge, attitude, character and support required to live triumphantly is key to fulfilling our destinies and overcoming challenges. Only when you are walking with God and in God can you begin to acquire that right knowledge required to live triumphantly. While answering the question on whose pain this book will be addressing, I stated that this book will be addressing the pain of all those who are challenged in one form or the other. In life, when we are faced with challenges, we usually wonder why we are the ones undergoing these challenges and not others rather than us. We tend to ask this question because we have failed or refused to see beyond our situation. If we will take out time to look pass these challenges, we will come to an understanding that what is presenting itself to us now as a challenge, has in fact done the same to others before us.

3.1 How Can Life Be Better Than What It Is Now?

Rather than waste our energy in wondering why we are the ones and not others, simply convert that energy into searching for solutions to how we can come out of the present dilemma. At other times, we may not be asking why we are the ones having the challenge and not others, our own questions might be, will I ever come out of this the same, or will this mean my end? I tell you; I may not have the answer to these questions, but you can decide that however it ends, you will come out with a positive and winning attitude to life.

a) You may or may not come out the same, but you must learn to live with the scars of life or seek solution as to how to remove the scars, if at all this is a possibility. You must build your resilience and faith enough to pull you through the challenging times, also select your social networks carefully, to have the right shoulders to lean on if necessary. When all is said and done, begin the rebuilding of your life piece by piece, remember that 'Rome was not built in a day', so take your time and focus on where you are headed, so you don't miss a step.

b) The question might be how do I cope with this? In life we all have different coping mechanisms when faced with a challenging situation, these mechanisms are suited and adaptable to our individual natures in life. So, you will have to determine and develop your own coping mechanisms in other to combat and triumph over your challenges. I find that taking solace in God is my own way of coping with my challenges, sometimes I seek advice and help from others depending on what the challenge is, but ultimately, I will always seek God's way to my situation before any other. You can determine how you wish to cope but have a winning attitude in focus.

c) How do people understand what I am going through? This might be your own question. I do not think it really matters if everyone understands what you are faced with, if the right people in your life understand. If nobody were to understand, if you are not deterred from your focus and resilience, you will be headed the right direction. However, the onus is on you to work towards making others understand the current situation of things with you. But bear in mind that not everyone will understand or give you the needed empathy as you may expect. Determine to relate with people on the same level they relate with your challenge or struggle.

Life is better when we say that it is, notwithstanding our current situation. Learning to be contented in all situations is key to forging ahead and finding the required strength and resilience to win over your challenges and live triumphantly.

3.2 Trusting in The Supernatural Ability of God

One thing I have come to realise over the years is that I am usually quick to comment about things that have to do with God. This stems from my deep trust, confidence and reliance on the supernatural ability of God Almighty to intervene in the affairs of humans, if we will grow our faith enough to trust Him. I am still learning and growing in this journey of trusting God the Father in all aspects of my life. You can learn to trust God with your affairs, desires and challenges. Know God for yourself, know His loving kindness and saving power, trust in His willingness to help you, if you would ask.

Patience is another area I like to talk about. When in life I find out that I am becoming impatient, it's usually because I am moving far from God, or I have stopped trusting in His help for that situation. However, this is not common with me, as I constantly strive to renew my trust in God daily. I have been through so much in life and have come out of so many challenges in life, that I can confidently say to you that this too shall pass, you will triumph if you hold on, remain focused and trust in God's love.

Challenges in life differ To some, theirs may be ill-health, to others it may be a lack in an area of their life and so on, but despite all these, God's purpose is that we come out victorious in our minds, our spirits, in our physical life and every area of life. God's love is so great, it does not discriminate. It does not matter what you have done, who you have become, or where you have been. The enormity of your sins is nothing compared to the love God has for you. If you decide to trust Him with the affairs of your life, you will enjoy His love, protection and provision.

CHAPTER 4

We All Have A Story

I was born and raised in Nigeria, to late retired soldier Amos Osho and his former wife, then Mrs Philomena Osho, both Nigerians. I lived most of my life in Nigeria, until I relocated to the United Kingdom in 2008. As a child I learnt to take God's words with full confidence, trusting in its ability to do what it says it will do. Sometimes I feel like it is taking too long to come to pass; but it eventually does come to pass at the end, it never falls. This attitude of trusting God against all odds, stems from having known Him alone as both my God and Daddy. I developed an intimate relationship with God from an early age but did not quite understand what it meant to be born again then, until later in my adult life.

4.1 Author's Story on How She Developed and Grew Her Resilience and Relationship with God

My parents separated when I was only three months old, my mother took me with her as I was still a breastfeeding baby and my older two siblings were left with my father. I was left with my late maternal grandmother, as my mother needed to go back to school in order to improve her financial status and be able to take care of us. When it was time for me to start schooling, according to my mother, she needed my father's tax clearance to register me in school, but due to the nature of my father's job, he was constantly redeployed and so could not be located. At that time, there were no emails, mobile telephones or any such communication network in Nigeria. Therefore, my mother had to register me with her own father's tax clearance which meant that she had to change my surname to her surname. All these happened to enable me to be accepted into any school.

I grow up believing that my maternal grandmother was my biological mother, we were very close and well bonded. A part of me gave way the day my maternal grandmother finally revealed to me that she was not my mother, but my grandmother. I had come to know and love my own mother like an eldest sister, I had always referred to her as big sister. Having to change that perspective was a herculean task and as a child, it was one of my first heartbreaks.

The next concern for me then was, now that my biological mother had been revealed to me, then, who is my father and where has he been all these years? Why haven't I met him yet, why has he not come looking for me and what is his name? Where did he come from, where is he now and what does he look like? These were some of the questions in my head as a child, so that when I am asked by someone, who is your father or how is your father? I used to say in my heart I wish I knew the answers. As the years went by, most of these questions were gradually answered and the gaps began to fill-up. However, one of the gaps just wasn't filling up and that was when do I finally meet my father or at least know what he looks like, sound like and the unending desire to call him my father. I wished and longed for the nostalgic feelings people have about their childhoods; especially other girls with their daddies; I wanted to feel same with my daddy.

That is where my relationship with my heavenly daddy started, knowing that God is my daddy and being able to always go back to God when I needed that daddy-daughter relationship. I faced my life and never felt alone or disadvantaged in life because I didn't grow up with my biological father, until it was time to get married. I had been bearing my maternal grandfather's surname all these while and had naturally assumed that he will give me away in marriage.

In Nigerian culture where I come from, we have what is called the traditional bride-price paying ceremony, where a woman's father and family gives her away to the fiancé, before she can be allowed to get married in church.

So, when it was time for me to get married, I went to inform my maternal grandfather about my fiancé and enquired from him on the way forward, knowing I had never met my biological father. As I was speaking with him, his wife (not my maternal grandmother), came out from the bedroom and said that I had better go and look for my biological father, or else my marriage dreams will crumble like a pack of cards. I tried to explain in a way that implied that since I have never met my father, I would not know where to start from. I also discussed the issue with my fiancé and his father, and they equally insisted that I should go and find my biological father. They stated that in their culture, a woman's bride-price is paid to her biological father. They also insisted that I change my surname from my maternal grandfather's surname to my biological father's surname before the marriage; to facilitate the change to my husband's surname, after our wedding.

At first, I was sceptical about going to search for my father, as I was not sure if I would be able to find him. But to my amazement, this venture opened a new chapter in my life and in my twenties, I found myself searching for my biological father, so he could give me away in marriage. I adventured out with the help and encouragement of my fiancé, who also accompanied me along, on the long journey, with a few other people. My mother provided me with adequate information to facilitate the search. It was undeniably an emotional moment when I eventually met my biological father for the first time. I had however, met my older siblings earlier.

I then needed to formally change my surname from my maternal grandfather's surname, back to my father's surname prior to our wedding, and eventually changed to my husband's surname after our wedding. The rest is history as they say and meeting my biological father drew me closer to God. I learned forgiveness, acceptance, obedience, love and the joy that comes from doing the will of God and obeying one's parents and elders. The Bible (KJV) says in Colossians 3:20 *"children, obey your parents in all things: for this is well pleasing unto the Lord"*. I understand that this verse is speaking to children. But I believe it can be applied to every younger person(s) who obeys and submits to the authority of the elders, whether the elder is a parent, grandparent, parent-in-law or others is irrelevant; it is God's will that we obey authorities. *"I am living the dream, because I was obedient to the call of the dream…"* – Oprah Winfrey.

I learnt to triumph over situations and circumstances of life. How to be resilient in the face of challenges; which has helped me in life's endeavours. Especially in my nineteen years of marriage, as I encountered initial delay in childbearing and suffered subsequent miscarriage, which further built my resilience until that prayer was answered and I gave birth to our child. I have always faced situations with a reflective mind-set, knowing that the God who has never allowed me to see shame, will not let me down now. Your story can end with joy too. Yes, you can be triumphant, keep working on yourself and building your resilience. Never forget to enjoy the good times. I make sure to celebrate the good times. Every day, I enjoy the goodness of God in my life and circumstances, I triumph daily.

CHAPTER 5

Resilience

Resilience helps us to keep going, to refuse to take no for an answer to our struggles, to reject failure and work for something better. Resilience is that inner strength we hold on to when every other strength has failed. It is what brings out the best in us, pushing us to scale the heights we would naturally have been afraid to climb. Resilience is needed in all spheres of life and we must constantly work on developing and mastering the act of being resilient.

5.1 What Is Resilience?

The Oxford dictionary defined resilience as *"the capacity to recover quickly from difficulties; toughness"*. Others have described resilience in different ways, here are a few of what they said. *"True resilience is much more than surviving the worst day of your life, it is about thriving every day of your life; we need resilience for many things, e.g. to raise a family, work a job, cope with stress, deal with ill-health, etc.; and just keep on going each day, the truth is that each of us can discover the strength we need most to become truly resilient"* – Rick Hanson, PhD., on his book "Resilient". *"Resilience means you cannot bounce back from hardship; you can only move through it"*, *"There is a path through pain to wisdom, through suffering to strength, and through fear to courage if we have the virtue of resilience"* – Eric Greitens, on his book "Resilience".

We have the capacity to be resilient, to want to try again when it seems we have done all we could and in the words of Barack Obama I say to you, "yes we can"!

Try again, try a different strategy, use a new method, but keep-on trying till you triumph, never accept no or failure for an answer and never give up on yourself or your dreams. *"In life, everybody has a turn-back moment, you have a moment when you could go forward, or you can give-up. But the thing you have to keep in mind before you give-up, is that if you give-up, the guarantee is that, it will never happen, that is the guarantee of quitting; that it will never happen, no way under the sun. The only way, the possibility remains that it will happen, is if you never give-up no matter what. Because, God is always coming, He is never too late"* – Steve Harvey.

5.2 Areas You Can Build Resilience

There are various areas you can build resilience, let us look at a few of these areas.

a) Build character, it takes character to listen and obey when you must. Character can open doors that you would not have been able to open ordinarily. In other words, 'your character determines your altitude' in live, your successes are as a result of your character and many other factors. As you succeed, you begin to build a team with people of like mind and character either in your personal life, at your place of work, place of study, with your spiritual congregation like a church or even in your social networking groups.

b) Work on your emotions, do not be quick to react in the face of situations and issues. Take time to ponder over event(s), analyse them and find ways around them before taking further actions, if possible. Your emotions may not always be the right one for the situation you are faced with, so, avoid making major decisions when you are emotional. You can cry or be angry if you must, but don't let your emotions cloud your senses, especially if you must make a judgement or a decision.

Deal with your feeling first by getting it under control, before going ahead with your actions and decisions. Especially if your decision(s) will affect others or yourself later or have a chain reaction in future. Choose to be a blessing to others and yourself, rather than nurse your wounded emotions. *"When it looked like the sun wasn't going to shine anymore...God put a rainbow in the clouds.*

Prepare yourself, so that you can be a rainbow in someone else's cloud, be a blessing to someone else" – Maya Angelou.

c) Be diligent in your work, whether it is your personal business you are running, or you are an employee, it is imperative that you are highly diligent and dedicated to your work. *"Hard work doesn't just appear; you have to practice hard work and grow in it"* – Michelle Obama. Be reliable, consistent and avoid lateness. Strive to be the best in what you do or at least to keep improving, be a team player, have the interest of the business in mind. Remember that you need resilience to do all these, so, continue to put it in focus. Having to get up every morning or go to work each time you must go, requires great dedication and resilience, which means that you will have to constantly draw from your inner strength and will-power in order to keep improving in what you do.

Diligence brings great opportunity and favour to the diligent, it may not be immediate, but it will surely bring you to limelight. The Bible in Proverbs 22:29 explains how the diligent comes to stand before kings; and not before mean men. My understanding of this means that the diligent always ends up favoured. Working smart is synonymous to being diligent or hard working, whilst also improving on yourself, enabling the opportunity for self-growth within your organisation or somewhere else. It is not enough to work hard if we are not doing the right thing, following the stipulated guidelines or we do not have any desire to keep improving on what we do. It is highly important to keep improving on what we do, by developing our skills, knowledge, ability and qualifications, in order to effect positive change to our growth within our line of work, business or in a different area of interest entirely.

d) Resilience is required to pursue academics, to fortify yourself against the challenges of academic deadlines, attendance and your own personal conflicts. As a student, you will need to be tough in the face of constant changes in academic requirements, standards, rules, regulations and stiff competitions. Remember to always put your goals in focus; work towards achieving that goal, which is to finish your studies within schedule and with a good grade. Prioritise your studies above your personal conflicts, take steps to map out your daily activities and ensure that you have enough time for your studies. Below are a few quotes of encouragement. *"Be the master of your fate"* – Oprah Winfrey. *"A habitude is strengthened whenever every action is repeated. For example, if you desire to be a polite person, have the habitude of being polite at first and then constantly"* – Eric Greitens, on his book "Resilience". Eric also talked about *"identity, action and feelings (I-A-F), which is explained like this: "Start with your identity, who do you want to be?, then take actions that are consistent with that identity, for example, if you want to be successful, then take actions that are synonymous with success, and be consistent with your actions. Finally, begin to feel like your identity"* – Brian Johnson describing Eric Greitens's, book "Resilience". *"Excellence is the most powerful answer you can give to the doubters and the haters, it is also the most powerful thing you can do for yourself"* – Michelle Obama.

e) In our personal and family lives, resilience is required to undergo the growth process (physical and mental), either in our lives or that of a family member. The ability to nurture a child from birth, till that child comes of age and becomes a responsible individual; who is both physically and mentally matured enough to stand on his or her own two feet, entails a great deal of resilience on your part and that of the child. Create time for family life, get together, listen to each other and know your individual personalities, strengths, weaknesses and desires/aspirations. Have a work-life balance, it is important to be diligent with your work, but not at the expense of your personal or family life.

Lookout for the interest of your family, make room for laughter, celebrate milestones and achievements, encourage and motivate one another, support each other by making up for their weaknesses. If you are a Christian, have a family altar where the family can always come together to offer their sacrifices of praise, worship, prayers and learn from the Holy Spirit as a family; where you can seek solutions for challenges and acquire strength to overcome and live triumphantly. Always be grateful to God for your family.

CHAPTER 6

Our Inner Strengths

Our inner strengths are the bedrocks and foundations upon which we can build and develop our resilience. Without working on these inner strengths, we may not have the sound or solid ground to build our resilience, develop a winning attitude that overcomes challenges or live a life of triumph. *"Grit, gratitude and compassion, these strengths are the key to resilience and the lasting wellbeing to a changing*

world" – Rick Hanson, PhD., on his book "Resilient". Let us look at some of the inner strengths required in building and developing our resilience:

6.1 How to Develop Resilience Through Working on Your Inner Strengths

Below are areas we can develop resilience by working on our inner strengths.

a) Gratitude is a great tool in the hand of the grateful, it allows the door of either natural or divine supply to remain open unto you. Your access to your provision and provider remains open if you remain appreciative. You block your access to your supply the moment you begin to exhibit ungratefulness. Lack of supply brings emptiness and failure and these works against resilience, because you will lack the self-will to keep trying due to consistent failures and emptiness. You may begin to wonder what is happening, the truth is you may have just blocked your access to your provision through ingratitude. Always be grateful for what you have and what you receive, learn to appreciate others and the role they play in your life.

Never belittle someone's help or gift to you, first show appreciation and then you can diplomatically ask for more if you must. Be grateful to God for life, many do not have the privilege of being alive or in their right mind, to enable them to be grateful to God, but you are able to, be thankful for that. Many will wish they are in your situation, always remember that there are others who are aspiring to be where you are now. Be grateful for your family - your parents, spouse, children and siblings; friends, neighbours, colleagues and everyone God places on your path in life. Appreciate them, constantly thank them for their role in your life and destiny. Doing this gives you the right and stable mindset, that shows you are well balanced in life and able to build relationships and it takes resilience to do so.

b) Compassion is an important virtue to have in our world today, it is something that is not quite common these days and yet highly important in our everyday life. We come across people and situations that need our compassion, but often, we are too busy or unconcerned to feel compassion for others and for ourselves sometimes. Being sympathetic to someone's misfortune or sufferings shows that you care and understand what they are going through and willing to empathise with them. The Bible in Luke 7:11-15, recorded a story about how Jesus felt compassion for a widow who lost her only son and was on her way to the burial, compassion moved our Lord Jesus to stop the procession and raised the man from the dead.

Compassion is a force that can help you go the extra mile for another person or yourself, where others have given up. It is also important to feel compassionate for oneself and work against becoming compassion fatigued. Most times we feel pity for others but not for ourselves. We must learn to forgive ourselves for our sufferings, especially if we have brought the misfortune on ourselves through wrong choices or decisions. Learning to forgive yourself and be compassionate to yourself is a key to building resilience, developing a winning attitude that overturns your challenges and sets you on the path to triumph.

There may be times where it is difficult to feel compassionate for oneself. For instance, someone in prison for breaking the law, who is now suffering due to that decision; may find it difficult to forgive or be compassionate to his or herself. Yet I can say to you that you are able to pick up the pieces of your life, if you decide that you are going to make a change. But you must start with being compassionate to yourself and then begin to build up what is left of your life through determination to change, and this can only be done through resilience and the fear of God. The Bible (KJV) said in Psalm 111:10a, that **"the fear of the Lord (God), is the beginning of wisdom"**; also in Job 28:28, it stated, *"and unto man he said, Behold, the fear of the Lord, that is wisdom; and to depart from evil is understanding"*. Remember it takes wisdom to bring about a positive change in one's life, as a foolish person cannot be able to bring about that positive change, so, decide to be compassionate to yourself and others by starting that positive change through your compassionate acts.

c) Joy is free and it is different from happiness, it is one of the fruits of the Holy Spirit as stated in the Bible (KJV), in Galatians 5:22-23 *"But the fruit of the Spirit is love, joy, peace, longsuffering, gentleness, goodness, faith, meekness, temperance: against such there is no law".* Unlike happiness which is determined by what we have achieved, acquired or have; joy is constant, it is a life style, a nature of ourselves and it does not reduce, diminish or die in the face of situations or achievements and it is a free gift from God.

Joy can be passive when we go through challenges and unpleasant situations, but it is never reduced diminished or dead. Joy is a solid ground on which to build resilience, because it is a strong force against challenges as it gives one the enabling inner strength to keep going, keep pushing until you win. Joy downsizes your challenges and reduces a problem, making it easier to face and conquer. We must ask God for the gift of joy in our lives, we must strive to make our joy contagious; as our joy can inspire others to want joy in their lives also.

Sharing in the joy of others is a good quality to have as it does not diminish your own joy but makes you appreciative of the work of God in another's live. Be careful and watch out for those things, triggers or people that may cause your joy to be dormant or passive and fight against them. The will of *God for us is to rejoice evermore, the Bible (KJV) says in Philippians 4:4, "Rejoice in the Lord always: and again, I say, Rejoice".* I encourage you to use your gift of joy daily in rejoicing over who and what you are now and who you will become in future.

d) Peace is also a fruit of the Holy Spirit. It is a state of rest, a period of tranquility in our mind, body or circumstances, it is a time we can achieve more as we are free from disruptions and distractions. God's will is for us to enjoy peace in this world that is full of disruptions and disturbances, and the only way of doing that is to remain focused on the cross of Christ and his finished work. Jesus said in John 14:27 *"Peace I leave with you, my peace I give unto you: not as the world giveth, give I unto you. Let not your heart be troubled, neither let it be afraid".*

Having the assurance of peace in our lives strengthens us to face the world and overcome. It is the ultimate foundation upon which we can grow our resilience and determination to live a life that triumphs over challenges. Peace is an inner strength that gives one the ability to think when others may be confused, this is peace of mind, when we are unperturbed with happenings about us or within us due to the inner peace we enjoy. When we are at peace, we can live with others around us peaceably and can contribute positively to our families and communities due to the deep-seated peace in our own lives. An unsettled person cannot bring peace to a situation, so we must be mindful of the fact that our peace is crucial to what we can achieve or become in life and therefore, guide our peace constantly.

e) Forgiveness is in two ways; one can ask for forgiveness or forgive others. It is a quality that enables us to coexist with others even after an offence. Without forgiveness, the world will be full of malice, divisions and unfulfilled dreams; because we can never fully realise our full potentials if we live under an atmosphere of unforgiveness. Unforgiveness can hinder one's blessings, In Matthew 6:12, Jesus taught his disciples how to pray effectively and one of the things He mentioned was forgiveness; He said we should ask God to forgive us our debts (trespasses, shortcomings), as we forgive our debtors. In other words, before we can access forgiveness from God, it is imperative that we also learn to forgive others also.

In my life story on how I grew and developed my resilience and relationship with God, I mentioned that forgiveness was one of the things I learned; I could not have moved forward in my relationship with both God Almighty or my biological father without forgiveness; I could not have accessed God's favours without forgiving my father for not being in my life earlier than he did. It will interest you to know that my father passed away a few years after I met him, what would have happened if I had disobeyed or delayed meeting him? I would never have had the privilege of forgiving him or giving him the opportunity of asking me for forgiveness. You may have someone who needs your forgiveness or maybe it is you who needs to ask for forgiveness, please do not wait till it is too late. Forgiveness is a great place to start in our journey of developing resilience, learning to forgive yourself, others and most importantly asking for forgiveness when you have wronged others is vital. The capacity to forgive is a force that stems from an inner strength, upon which we can build resilience.

All that is required is to make that decision to forgive or ask for forgiveness and then take the necessary steps to actualise the decision.

f) Acceptance is defined by the Oxford dictionary as *"the action of consenting to receive or undertake something offered, the process or fact of being received as adequate, valid, or suitable".* Acceptance is easy to effect when it is what we expect, desire, or dimmed-fit, but most often, acceptance is forced on us and it is usually things that we are unable to change that we learn to accept. Acceptance is that point at which we decide to tolerate something or a situation willingly, because we are unable to effect any change in that regards.

For example, accepting the imposed lockdown on us due to the current situation with COVID-19 in the world, is a clear instance of inability to change a situation and so, learn to leave with it for as long as is necessary. Getting to the point of acceptance helps us to forge-ahead in an already difficult situation, enabling us to develop the resilience required to overcome that situation or challenge and triumph in our goal. (I want to use this opportunity and privilege to pray for as many that are currently sick with COVID-19 and other illnesses, all over the world. I pray that God intervenes in their situations and grant them perfect health in Jesus name. For those who may have lost a love one, I pray for comfort for you and your families, may the almighty God succour you, in Jesus name).

A long time ago I came across an anonymous prayer called the serenity prayer, which goes like this: *God grant me the serenity to ACCEPT the things I cannot change, COURAGE to change the things I can, and WISDOM to know the difference.* Accepting the things, we are unable to change, brings us a renewed peace of mind and joy that we finally can move forward, regardless of what the new norm may be. Bear in mind that accepting something we are unable to change is not the same as settling for less or accepting failure or defeat. Rather the ability to say to yourself, that you have done all there is to be done, within your power and will now move on with what is left of the situation, that is not within your human ability to change, though you would have preferred a change. Learn to accept the good and the positives and reject the bad and the negatives, provided it is within your power to do so. If you must accept what you cannot change, make sure it is not within human capability to change it.

g) Love is another fruit of the spirit and the very essence and nature of God. The Bible (KJV), says in 1 John 4:8 *"He that loveth not knoweth not God; for God is love"*. It also says in Genesis 1:27 that God made us in His own image and likeness. Which to me means, that we are an embodiment of God's nature, which is love; therefore, we are capable of loving people and we can show love to others unconditionally if we choose to do so. Who or what you love you will not hurt or harm; love, being an affectionate feeling helps us to take pleasure in those people or what we love. "Life without love is like a tree without blossoms or fruit" Anonymous.

This deep feeling of affection for others or things, goes a long way in helping us to remain focused in the face of challenges, bringing us hope that we can win and surmount that challenge if we try harder. It pushes us forward till we overcome the challenge, enabling us to redirect our energy into loving our object of affection. *"The power of hope, the belief that something better is always possible if you are willing to work for it and fight for it"* – Michelle Obama.

Love brings hope into a difficult situation and equips us to fight on and go through it without giving up; most times we go on because we want to do it for ourselves and those we love. It is important that we love God from whom we all inherited the nature of love; also show love to your family, friends and people in general. Exercise your power of love; do not allow it to be dormant, showing unconditional love to others shows that you are mentally capable of building solid relationships and handling challenges.

Learn to love yourself; it is vital that you appreciate who God created you to be, know that you are unique and special. When we love ourselves, we begin to discover the hidden or inner qualities that God has deposited within us and use them to our advantage, these strengths support us to live a life of triumph and victory all through our lifetime. *"The strongest force in human personality is the need to remain consistent with how we see ourselves".* *"The image we hold of ourselves controls our successes and our failures and impacts every single area of our lives"*– Dan Lok.

It is highly impossible to love others if we do not see anything lovable within ourselves. When we feel that there is nothing of value in us, we open the door of depression and gloom; which in turn works against our ability to develop the winning attitudes required for overcoming challenges, building resilience and triumphing in life. Love is a good quality or virtue to have. Pray for it, apply it in your life, use it on others and continue to develop the act of loving unconditionally.

h) Courage is the ability to venture into something you would have otherwise been afraid of doing. I have heard that courage is not the absence of fear, but the ability to go on despite that fear. Courage is what enables us to face a situation or circumstance and not be afraid of it, but rather face it until we have dealt with it and triumphed over it. It is a quality or virtue that everyone who aspires to be something or someone in life must possess. We need courage and the grace of God to make the right choices in life and to live with our choices. Stepping out into your dreams and goals in life requires huge courage and you must work against everything that frightens you from taking that first step.

Practice courage in all you do and be consistent with it, as that is the only way to keep pushing yourself forward in order to achieve your goals in life. *"Courage is the most important of all the virtues, because without courage you can't practice any other virtue consistently. You can be consistently kind or fair or humane but not without courage, because sooner or later you will stop and say the threat is too much, the difficulty is too high, the challenge is too great"* – Maya Angelou.

Courage can set you apart from others, it can promote you faster than those who would not dare to try, it will keep you going, pushing and believing when everything else has failed. Develop your courage by constantly challenging yourself to do those things that take you out of your comfort zone.

For in doing them, you advance and build your resilience, whilst achieving a winning attitude for triumphing above any challenges.

6.2 Conclusion

Having considered how we can develop resilience by working on our inner strengths, it therefore beholds on us to keep working on these strengths and virtues for the remainder of our lives. Life is a constant battle and we must make it a victorious and triumphant war for ourselves. We can only aspire to achieve this by not giving-up in the face of difficulties, challenges and barriers. Doing those things that enhances your development in a positive way and gives you the ability to perceive, focus and be at alert to respond adequately to any barriers are crucial to winning the battles of life.

Be principled and remain so, never settle for anything less than what you believe in, aspire for or work hard for; never bend the rules for anyone and make up your mind to stay on the right path. *"The man who changes his principles easily, depending on who he is dealing with, is not a man who can lead a nation"* – Nelson Mandela. Do not allow yourself to be influenced by negativity, self-doubt, or be too complacent. Set goals on what you intend to achieve next, what you want to do next and who you wish to become in the immediate future.

Concentrate on achieving your goals and when you succeed, use the success to advance your cause, empower yourself, bless humanity, serve God and quench the longings of your soul. *"Authentic power is when your personality comes to serve the energy of your soul, when you are able to align who you are, who you have become in the world, with really what you have come to do in the world, when your personality serves the soul"* - Oprah Winfrey describing Gary Zukav 's book- Seed of the soul.

Life is beautiful and we can live it without battles and wars, we must learn to celebrate life daily and enjoy the free gifts of God. Be grateful for life, for all you are and aspire to be. But when life releases the negative, in the form of challenges, it becomes imperative that we are prepared, equipped and ready to draw strength from within us, in order to triumph over the challenges.

However, if we happen to be in a good place now, where we currently do not have any challenges, then it is even more important that we strive to keep it as it is and work hard at keeping that door against negative forces shut. The Holy Spirit will help us, all we need do is ask, trust and believe.

Thank You All!

I want to use this opportunity and privilege to thank the Almighty God, my Heavenly Daddy, for His inspiration, grace and enablement; given me to be able to write this book and making me useful in His hands to affect lives positively. I am grateful for being an instrument of salvation to many that will read this book and an encourager to those who wants to utilise their inner strengths and right attitudes in reordering their realms of existence and overcoming the vicissitudes of life through the help of the Holy Spirit.

My heartfelt thanks go to my darling husband Winston Ugono, for your love and support. Thank you for being my greatest encourager.

I want to also acknowledge my mother, Philomena Ogwudiegwu, for giving me the opportunity of becoming who I am today. God bless you Mummy! To my four siblings, I say thank you for being my family. To my father, I say continue to rest in peace daddy.

My special thanks go to pastor Chris Gbenle (the provincial pastor in my local church), for writing the foreword of this book. I am also grateful to pastor Afolabi Otitoju for helping with the editing of this book, you are awesome sir. Also thanking Florence Igboayaka for helping me fulfil my dreams of writing a book, you brought out my hidden potential and made this happen.

To my launch team I say a big thank you, for going on this journey with me. You all made it happen. Special thanks to David Emele, Lolade Okunrinboye, Ifeoma Umez and Lanle Ayansina. To everyone who reviewed this book at some point, I same a big thank you. I am grateful to you all.

And thank you the reader for purchasing and reading this book. May God answer all your prayers and meet you at the point of your needs, in Jesus name, amen.

Rosemary Ugono

www.ingramcontent.com/pod-product-compliance
Lightning Source LLC
Chambersburg PA
CBHW071508030726
47593CB00003B/1214